This journal belongs to:

_____

_____

_____

# My Prayer Journey

———

A 52-WEEK GUIDED JOURNAL
*to* INSPIRE A DEEPER CONNECTION
WITH GOD

Ink &
Willow

Behold the Throne of Grace!
The Promise calls me near;
There Jesus shows his smiling face;
And waits to answer prayer.

That rich atoning blood
Which, sprinkled round, I see,
Provides for those who come to God
An all-prevailing plea.

My soul, ask what thou wilt,
Thou canst not be too bold;
Since his own blood for thee he spilt,
What else can he withhold?

Beyond thy utmost wants
His love and power can bless.
To praying souls he always grants
More than they can express.

JOHN NEWTON, 1779

# CONTENTS

# HOW TO USE THIS BOOK

*THERE IS POWER IN PRAYER.* Through it, we ask God to soften hearts, incite miracles, and calm our souls. Stories of prayer's life-changing impact abound, whether from the far corners of the earth or the neighbor down the street. We may even have a personal story or two to share. Yet prayer doesn't come easy. We may struggle to find the words, feel inadequate, or even battle with consistency in our prayer life. Promises to pray are easy to pass out but harder to keep, as this spiritual discipline takes a back seat to the busyness of life. We have great intentions for our prayer lives, but at times we fall short. This guided journal will help you grasp hold of those good intentions and dive deep into your prayer life.

## PRAYER REQUEST LOG

The Prayer Request Log on pages 9–19 is an organized, simple way to keep track of every specific concern or request you've taken to God in prayer, with space to record His answers. You'll never again forget a promise to pray for a friend or loved one, and you'll be encouraged to trust God's faithfulness and provision.

In the pages that follow, you'll find fifty-two weekly prayer journal spreads, allowing you to record your prayerful thoughts and requests for a full year. Each week you are invited to focus your time with God by responding to the following prompts:

I am thankful for . . .

I am worried about . . .

I am praying for . . .

## BONUS FEATURES

Containing inspiring devotional insights, encouraging quotes and Scriptures, as well as suggested prayer practices, *My Prayer Journey* offers new ways to pray "without ceasing." Additional features include an inspirational playlist (also available on Spotify), stories behind beloved hymns and prayers, and thoughtful journaling prompts.

✝ ✝ ✝

We pray this journal will give you space to express your hardships, praises, and concerns to God, as you find new ways to pray confidently, continuously, and consistently. In doing so, may you discover anew God's supernatural peace and presence.

# PRAYER REQUEST LOG

| Date | Prayer Request | How Did God Answer Your Prayer? |
| --- | --- | --- |
| | | |
| | | |
| | | |
| | | |
| | | |
| | | |
| | | |
| | | |
| | | |

| Date | Prayer Request | How Did God Answer Your Prayer? |
| --- | --- | --- |
|  |  |  |
|  |  |  |
|  |  |  |
|  |  |  |
|  |  |  |
|  |  |  |
|  |  |  |
|  |  |  |
|  |  |  |
|  |  |  |

| Date | Prayer Request | How Did God Answer Your Prayer? |
|------|----------------|--------------------------------|
|      |                |                                |
|      |                |                                |
|      |                |                                |
|      |                |                                |
|      |                |                                |
|      |                |                                |
|      |                |                                |
|      |                |                                |
|      |                |                                |
|      |                |                                |

| Date | Prayer Request | How Did God Answer Your Prayer? |
| --- | --- | --- |
| | | |
| | | |
| | | |
| | | |
| | | |
| | | |
| | | |
| | | |
| | | |
| | | |

| Date | Prayer Request | How Did God Answer Your Prayer? |
|------|----------------|--------------------------------|
|      |                |                                |
|      |                |                                |
|      |                |                                |
|      |                |                                |
|      |                |                                |
|      |                |                                |
|      |                |                                |
|      |                |                                |
|      |                |                                |
|      |                |                                |

| Date | Prayer Request | How Did God Answer Your Prayer? |
| --- | --- | --- |
| | | |
| | | |
| | | |
| | | |
| | | |
| | | |
| | | |
| | | |
| | | |
| | | |

| Date | Prayer Request | How Did God Answer Your Prayer? |
|------|----------------|----------------------------------|
|      |                |                                  |
|      |                |                                  |
|      |                |                                  |
|      |                |                                  |
|      |                |                                  |
|      |                |                                  |
|      |                |                                  |
|      |                |                                  |
|      |                |                                  |
|      |                |                                  |

| Date | Prayer Request | How Did God Answer Your Prayer? |
| --- | --- | --- |
| | | |
| | | |
| | | |
| | | |
| | | |
| | | |
| | | |
| | | |
| | | |

| Date | Prayer Request | How Did God Answer Your Prayer? |
|------|----------------|--------------------------------|
|      |                |                                |
|      |                |                                |
|      |                |                                |
|      |                |                                |
|      |                |                                |
|      |                |                                |
|      |                |                                |
|      |                |                                |
|      |                |                                |
|      |                |                                |

| Date | Prayer Request | How Did God Answer Your Prayer? |
|------|----------------|--------------------------------|
|      |                |                                |
|      |                |                                |
|      |                |                                |
|      |                |                                |
|      |                |                                |
|      |                |                                |
|      |                |                                |
|      |                |                                |
|      |                |                                |
|      |                |                                |

| Date | Prayer Request | How Did God Answer Your Prayer? |
|---|---|---|
| | | |
| | | |
| | | |
| | | |
| | | |
| | | |
| | | |
| | | |
| | | |
| | | |

*WEEK*

1

## I am thankful for...

_____

_____

_____

_____

_____

_____

_____

_____

_____

_____

_____

_____

_____

_____

_____

_____

_____

I am worried about…

_____

_____

_____

_____

_____

_____

_____

_____

I am praying for…

_____

_____

_____

_____

_____

_____

_____

_____

*WEEK*

2

I am thankful for…

# I am worried about...

_____

_____

_____

_____

_____

_____

_____

# I am praying for...

_____

_____

_____

_____

_____

_____

_____

_____

Prayer is both conversation and encounter with God.

TIMOTHY KELLER

# Scripture Meditation

*SCRIPTURE MEDITATION CAN BE A POWERFUL WAY* to focus your mind on the truth in God's Word. Donald S. Whitney wrote in his book *Spiritual Disciplines for the Christian Life*, "As opposed to daydreaming wherein you let your mind wander, with meditation you focus your thoughts. You give your attention to the verse, phrase, word, or teaching of Scripture you have chosen. Instead of mental aimlessness, in meditation your mind is on a track—it's going somewhere; it has direction."[1]

Spend a few minutes meditating on Romans 8:35–39 and then identify three insights that apply to an issue or question with which you are currently struggling.

INSIGHT ONE

_____

_____

INSIGHT TWO

_____

_____

INSIGHT THREE

_____

_____

Who shall separate us from the love of Christ? Shall trouble or hardship or persecution or famine or nakedness or danger or sword? As it is written: "For your sake we face death all day long; we are considered as sheep to be slaughtered." No, in all these things we are more than conquerors through him who loved us. For I am convinced that neither death nor life, neither angels nor demons, neither the present nor the future, nor any powers, neither height nor depth, nor anything else in all creation, will be able to separate us from the love of God that is in Christ Jesus our Lord.
*(Romans 8:35–39)*

*WEEK*

# 3

## I am thankful for…

_____

_____

_____

_____

_____

_____

_____

_____

_____

_____

_____

_____

_____

_____

_____

_____

_____

I am worried about...

_____

_____

_____

_____

_____

_____

_____

_____

I am praying for...

_____

_____

_____

_____

_____

_____

_____

*WEEK*

4

I am thankful for...

## I am worried about…

_____

_____

_____

_____

_____

_____

_____

_____

## I am praying for…

_____

_____

_____

_____

_____

_____

_____

_____

_____

*WEEK*
5

## I am thankful for…

_____

_____

_____

_____

_____

_____

_____

_____

_____

_____

_____

_____

_____

_____

_____

I am worried about...

_____

_____

_____

_____

_____

_____

_____

_____

I am praying for...

_____

_____

_____

_____

_____

_____

_____

# Write Your Own Song

*MUSIC IS POWERFUL.* When we hear a familiar or much-loved song, it can shape our day, bring forth memories, and grant words to express our emotions. Similarly, worship songs and hymns can be a wonderful way to prepare our souls for prayer since they remind us of God's goodness, help us verbalize our heartache or longings, and point us back to the character of God. In the space below, try composing an original song or a new stanza for one of your favorite hymns. For inspiration, listen to some of the songs from the list on the next page.

"AMAZING GRACE" *by Aretha Franklin*

"TRUST IN YOU" *by Lauren Daigle*

"I'LL FIND YOU" *by LeCrae and Tori Kelly*

"COME AWAKE" *by David Crowder Band*

"PRAY" *by Sanctus Real*

"10,000 REASONS" *by Matt Redman*

"YOU ARE MY VISION" *by Rend Collective*

"SEE YOU AGAIN" *by Anthony Evans*

"HOW GREAT THOU ART" *by Carrie Underwood and Vince Gill*

"TOUCH THE HEM OF HIS GARMENT" *by Sam Cooke and The Soul Stirrers*

"HALLELUJAH, YOU ARE GOOD" *(feat. Matt Maher) by Steven Curtis Chapman*

"IN CHRIST ALONE" *by Keith & Kristyn Getty and Alison Krauss*

"MORE THAN CONQUERORS" *by Rend Collective*

"YOUR SPIRIT" *(feat. Kierra Sheard) by Tasha Cobb Leonard*

"BE STILL AND KNOW" *by Amy Grant*

"BY YOUR SIDE" *by Tenth Avenue North*

"WHEN WE PRAY" *by Tauren Wells*

"HOLY, HOLY, HOLY" *by Audrey Assad*

"SAFE" *by Phil Wickham*

"DOWN TO THE RIVER TO PRAY" *by Alison Krauss*

"AMAZING GRACE (MY CHAINS ARE GONE)" *by Chris Tomlin*

"MULTIPLIED" *by NEEDTOBREATHE*

THIS PLAYLIST INSPIRES BOTH PRAYER AND PRAISE. CONTAINING HYMNS AND CLASSIC CHRISTIAN SONGS ALONGSIDE MORE MODERN WORSHIP ANTHEMS, THE PLAYLIST IS AVAILABLE ON SPOTIFY AT WMBOOKS.COM/ GIFTOFPRAYERPLAYLIST.

*WEEK*
# 6

## I am thankful for...

_____

_____

_____

_____

_____

_____

_____

_____

_____

_____

_____

_____

_____

_____

_____

I am worried about...

_____
_____
_____
_____
_____
_____
_____
_____
_____

I am praying for...

_____
_____
_____
_____
_____
_____
_____
_____
_____

*WEEK*
7

I am thankful for...

_____
_____
_____
_____
_____
_____
_____
_____
_____
_____
_____
_____
_____
_____
_____
_____

# I am worried about...

_____

_____

_____

_____

_____

_____

_____

_____

# I am praying for...

_____

_____

_____

_____

_____

_____

_____

_____

# Discovering the Practice of Prayer

PRAYER HAS BEEN A PART OF MY LIFE for as long as I can remember—prayer before meals, before bed, while in church—but it wasn't until I was a college student that I really began to appreciate prayer as a practice. Whether you're familiar with the concept or not, consider trying one of the prayer practices below. These methods might seem formal or rigid, but over time, they can become the stepping-stones to an intentional life of prayer.

1 | **Lectio Divina**, which is Latin for *divine reading*, is a Benedictine practice that combines Bible reading, meditation, and prayer to deepen spiritual growth and communion with God.

   ✛ Choose a Bible passage and *read* it carefully several times.

   ✛ *Meditate* or journal on what the Holy Spirit is saying to you.

   ✛ *Pray* through anything God may be teaching you through the passage.

   ✛ *Rest* in silence while you contemplate the message and the specific ways you can live it out.

2 | When you don't have any of your own words, simply choose a **prayer or promise** recorded in the Bible and pray through it. You can even substitute your own name for added emphasis. The following is an example of this, using the beginning of Psalm 23 (ESV).

The Lord is _____'s shepherd; she shall not want. He makes her lie down in green pastures. He leads her beside still waters. He restores her soul . . .

3 | Change your **physical posture** to reflect your spiritual attitude. Try sitting with your forearms on your knees so your palms face the floor. Release in prayer whatever distractions, worries, or frustrations are weighing on your heart. Then turn your palms faceup and, now that your hands are "empty," ask God to fill you with peace, strength, or anything you might need.

4 | **Repetition of Scriptural truth** can be another important exercise in your prayer life. To focus your mind, choose a short verse and synchronize each line with an inhalation and an exhalation. Try this technique with Psalm 46:10 and repeat four or five times to engage a prayerful mindset:

**On an in-breath:** Be still and know

**On an out-breath:** that I am God.

*WEEK*

8

# I am thankful for...

_____

_____

_____

_____

_____

_____

_____

_____

_____

_____

_____

_____

_____

_____

_____

I am worried about...

_____
_____
_____
_____
_____
_____
_____
_____

I am praying for...

_____
_____
_____
_____
_____
_____
_____
_____

*WEEK*
9

## I am thankful for...

_____

_____

_____

_____

_____

_____

_____

_____

_____

_____

_____

_____

_____

_____

_____

_____

_____

I am worried about…

_____

_____

_____

_____

_____

_____

_____

I am praying for…

_____

_____

_____

_____

_____

_____

_____

*WEEK*
# 10

## I am thankful for...

I am worried about...

_____
_____
_____
_____
_____
_____
_____
_____
_____

I am praying for...

_____
_____
_____
_____
_____
_____
_____
_____
_____

For the Spirit God gave us does not make us timid,
but gives us power, love and self-discipline.

2 TIMOTHY 1:7


Fear of man will prove to be a snare,
    but whoever trusts in the LORD is kept safe.

PROVERBS 29:25


Do not be anxious about anything, but in everything
by prayer and supplication with thanksgiving let your
requests be made known to God. And the peace of God,
which surpasses all understanding, will guard your hearts
and your minds in Christ Jesus.

PHILIPPIANS 4:6–7, ESV


Humble yourselves, therefore, under God's mighty hand,
that he may lift you up in due time. Cast all your anxiety
on him because he cares for you.

1 PETER 5:6–7


Say to those who have an anxious heart,
    "Be strong; fear not!
Behold, your God
    will come with vengeance,
with the recompense of God.
    He will come and save you."

ISAIAH 35:4, ESV

Peace I leave with you; my peace I give you. I do not give to you as the world gives. Do not let your hearts be troubled and do not be afraid.

JOHN 14:27

I sought the LORD, and he answered me;
    he delivered me from all my fears.

PSALM 34:4

The LORD your God is in your midst,
    a mighty one who will save;
he will rejoice over you with gladness;
    he will quiet you by his love;
he will exult over you with loud singing.

ZEPHANIAH 3:17, ESV

Let the peace of Christ rule in your hearts, since as members of one body you were called to peace. And be thankful.

COLOSSIANS 3:15

Come to me, all you who are weary and burdened, and I will give you rest. Take my yoke upon you and learn from me, for I am gentle and humble in heart, and you will find rest for your souls. For my yoke is easy and my burden is light.

MATTHEW 11:28–30

*WEEK*
11

I am thankful for…

_____

_____

_____

_____

_____

_____

_____

_____

_____

_____

_____

_____

_____

_____

_____

_____

_____

_____

# I am worried about...

_____

_____

_____

_____

_____

_____

_____

_____

# I am praying for...

_____

_____

_____

_____

_____

_____

_____

_____

*WEEK*

## 12

I am thankful for...

I am worried about…

_____

_____

_____

_____

_____

_____

_____

_____

_____

I am praying for…

_____

_____

_____

_____

_____

_____

_____

_____

_____

Let others say what
they will of the
efficacy of prayer,
I believe in it,
and I shall pray.
Thank God!
Yes, I shall always pray.

SOJOURNER TRUTH

## *Concentric Circles*

*DO YOU STRUGGLE TO KNOW HOW TO PRAY?* Do you run out of things to pray after only a few minutes? One prayer practice that might be valuable is to pray in concentric circles, starting with yourself and then moving outward to your family, then to your close friends, from there to your coworkers or church family, and out to the wider circles of your city, state, and nation, and ultimately to the social or cultural issues in the world. Even if you can't pray through every circle every day, this pattern of prayer will equip you to structure your time with God more effectively.[2]

SELF

FAMILY

FRIENDS

COWORKERS

CITY/STATE

NATION

WORLD

*WEEK*
13

## I am thankful for...

_____
_____
_____
_____
_____
_____
_____
_____
_____
_____
_____
_____
_____
_____
_____
_____
_____
_____

I am worried about...

_____

_____

_____

_____

_____

_____

_____

_____

I am praying for...

_____

_____

_____

_____

_____

_____

_____

_____

*WEEK*
14

I am thankful for...

# I am worried about...

_____

_____

_____

_____

_____

_____

_____

_____

# I am praying for...

_____

_____

_____

_____

_____

_____

_____

_____

*WEEK*
15

# I am thankful for…

# I am worried about...

_____

_____

_____

_____

_____

_____

_____

_____

# I am praying for...

_____

_____

_____

_____

_____

_____

_____

_____

# The Language of Prayer

*SOME HOLY WORDS HAVE BEEN SO OVERUSED IN PRAYER* and in Christian culture that they have lost some of their meaning or significance. The result is that we speak these words without truly recognizing their application to or presence in our own lives.

Reflect on the words below and write down a sentence or two to describe what they mean to you and your prayer life.

1 | PRAYER

_____

_____

_____

2 | MEDITATION

_____

_____

_____

3 | REFLECTION

_____

_____

_____

4 | PEACE

_____

_____

_____

## 5 | GRACE

_____

_____

_____

## 6 | LAMENT

_____

_____

_____

## 7 | FORGIVENESS

_____

_____

_____

## 8 | INTERCESSION

_____

_____

_____

## 9 | PRAISE

_____

_____

_____

## 10 | CONFESSION

_____

_____

_____

*WEEK*
16

I am thankful for...

# I am worried about...

_____

_____

_____

_____

_____

_____

_____

_____

# I am praying for...

_____

_____

_____

_____

_____

_____

_____

_____

*WEEK*

17

I am thankful for...

I am worried about...

_____

_____

_____

_____

_____

_____

_____

_____

I am praying for...

_____

_____

_____

_____

_____

_____

_____

_____

We must lay
before him
what is in us;
not what ought
to be in us.

C. S. LEWIS

*SOMETIMES, OUR PRAYERS ARE ROUTINE. God, bless this food, make it healthy to our bodies.* Sometimes, they are short and to the point. For example, the alarm didn't go off and we're racing to start the day, so our prayer reflects that urgency. *God, clear the roads on my way to work.*

At other times, anger and hurt harden our hearts, and we feel as though our prayers have become a one-sided conversation. Our pain is not easily dismissed, but instead twists our guts into a knot so tight we are at a loss for breath. The anger we feel burns like a fire in our souls, in danger of festering into a grudge that can last years. In the midst of these all-encompassing moments, let David's words echo in your mind: "Enter his gates with thanksgiving, and his courts with praise! Give thanks to him; bless his name!" (Psalm 100:4, ESV).

An unexpected thing happens when we name the things we appreciate: our attitude shifts. Instead of focusing on our anger, we begin to recognize God's blessings. Instead of pain, we feel gratitude and love because of His care for us. Our hearts soften and our perception of the situation changes. Our mood brightens as we recognize the artistry in His work. His character and promises shine through the dark cloud over us. The knot in our chest begins to unravel and we feel His peace. At last we can proclaim,

> For the LORD is good;
> his steadfast love endures forever,
> and his faithfulness to all generations. *(Psalm 100:5, ESV)*

With our hearts primed in thanksgiving, the words begin to flow. We fall to our knees and express our pain. We pour out our anger at His feet. He sees us and hears our prayer. In Him, we have a confidant, a comforter, a healer. Praise be to God.

*WEEK*

# 18

## I am thankful for…

I am worried about...

_____
_____
_____
_____
_____
_____
_____
_____
_____

I am praying for...

_____
_____
_____
_____
_____
_____
_____
_____
_____

*WEEK*
19

I am thankful for...

_____

_____

_____

_____

_____

_____

_____

_____

_____

_____

_____

_____

_____

_____

_____

_____

_____

_____

# I am worried about...

_____

_____

_____

_____

_____

_____

_____

_____

# I am praying for...

_____

_____

_____

_____

_____

_____

_____

_____

_____

*WEEK*
## 20

# I am thankful for...

_____

_____

_____

_____

_____

_____

_____

_____

_____

_____

_____

_____

_____

_____

_____

_____

I am worried about...

_____
_____
_____
_____
_____
_____
_____
_____

I am praying for...

_____
_____
_____
_____
_____
_____
_____
_____

# The Story Behind the Hymn

"*BE THOU MY VISION*" *EXEMPLIFIES THE CONVERGENCE* of lyrics and melody across the centuries to shape one of today's most beautiful hymns in any language. Derived from the eighth-century Irish folk song "Slane," the Old Irish text was put to music in the early 1900s. It is said that Saint Patrick lit a bonfire on Easter Eve on Slane Hill, County Meath, Ireland. This was in defiance of the decree by High King Logaire of Tara that no fire could be lit before the king signaled the beginning of the pagan Spring Equinox festival of Ostara. Despite his defiance, High King Logaire was so impressed by Patrick's devotion to his faith that he allowed Ireland's first Christian missionary to continue his work.

Saint Patrick (c. 385–461), born in what is now modern-day England, belonged to a family heavily influenced by the Roman Empire and its culture. He grew up surrounded by deep Christian traditions, but his own approach to faith remained minimal until a pivotal moment—his capture and enslavement by Irish Druids. During his six years as a slave, he gained an insider's perspective on the Druid people and their way of life. More important, he developed a keen awareness of the truth of the gospel and experienced a complete life transformation.

Years later, after returning to Britain and pastoring a community there for almost twenty years, he felt an urgent call to minister to the Druid "barbarians." Because of his thorough knowledge of their culture and traditions, his mission work among them thrived, to the point that he eventually became Ireland's patron saint.[3]

This simple prayer of Celtic Christian origin, now a contemporary hymn, reminds us that although our path may be unclear at times, Christ is always near us and for us.

# Be Thou My Vision

Be Thou my Vision, O Lord of my heart;
Naught be all else to me, save that Thou art;
Thou my best Thought, by day or by night,
Waking or sleeping, Thy presence my light.

Be Thou my Wisdom, and Thou my true Word;
I ever with Thee and Thou with me, Lord;
Thou my great Father, I Thy true son;
Thou in me dwelling, and I with Thee one.

Be Thou my battle Shield, Sword for the fight;
Be Thou my Dignity, Thou my Delight;
Thou my soul's Shelter, Thou my high Tow'r:
Raise Thou me heav'nward, O Pow'r of my pow'r.

Riches I heed not, nor man's empty praise,
Thou mine Inheritance, now and always:
Thou and Thou only, first in my heart,
High King of Heaven, my Treasure Thou art.

High King of Heaven, my victory won,
May I reach Heaven's joys, O bright Heav'n's Sun!
Heart of my own heart, whatever befall,
Still be my Vision, O Ruler of all.

———————

DALLAN FORGAILL (530–598),

TRANSLATED BY MARY ELIZABETH BYRNE (1880–1931)

*WEEK*
## 21

## I am thankful for...

_____

_____

_____

_____

_____

_____

_____

_____

_____

_____

_____

_____

_____

_____

_____

# I am worried about…

_____

_____

_____

_____

_____

_____

_____

_____

# I am praying for…

_____

_____

_____

_____

_____

_____

_____

_____

*WEEK*
## 22

## I am thankful for…

_____

_____

_____

_____

_____

_____

_____

_____

_____

_____

_____

_____

_____

_____

_____

_____

_____

_____

I am worried about...

_____
_____
_____
_____
_____
_____
_____
_____

I am praying for...

_____
_____
_____
_____
_____
_____
_____
_____

"Prayer was never meant
to be magic," Mother said.
"Then why bother with it?"
Suzy scowled.
"Because it's an act of love."

————

MADELEINE L'ENGLE

# A.C.T.S.

*ONE OF THE CLASSIC CHRISTIAN APPROACHES TO PRACTICING* prayer is to use the acrostic A.C.T.S. as a guide. Each letter stands for a key element of prayer: *A* for adoration, *C* for confession, *T* for thanksgiving, and *S* for supplication. According to the late R. C. Sproul, a well-known pastor and author, "not only does this acrostic remind us of the elements of prayer, it shows us the priority we ought to give to each."[4] During your next prayer time, try this approach. Begin by spending time praising God, expressing your adoration for His provision and care. Next, confess your fears and failures to the Lord, acknowledging that you have fallen short. Then thank God for His everlasting grace and mercy. Finally, present your requests to the Lord, outlining your needs or the needs of others.

*WEEK*

## 23

I am thankful for...

I am worried about...

_____
_____
_____
_____
_____
_____
_____
_____

I am praying for...

_____
_____
_____
_____
_____
_____
_____
_____

*WEEK*
24

I am thankful for...

_____

_____

_____

_____

_____

_____

_____

_____

_____

_____

_____

_____

_____

_____

_____

_____

I am worried about...

_____

_____

_____

_____

_____

_____

_____

_____

I am praying for...

_____

_____

_____

_____

_____

_____

_____

_____

_____

*WEEK*
25

# I am thankful for...

I am worried about...

_____

_____

_____

_____

_____

_____

_____

I am praying for...

_____

_____

_____

_____

_____

_____

_____

We are happy because of the hope we have of sharing God's glory. We also have joy with our troubles, because we know that these troubles produce patience. And patience produces character, and character produces hope. And this hope will never disappoint us, because God has poured out his love to fill our hearts.

ROMANS 5:2–5, NCV

Those who hope in the LORD
    will renew their strength.
They will soar on wings like eagles;
    they will run and not grow weary,
    they will walk and not be faint.

ISAIAH 40:31

"For I know the plans I have for you," declares the LORD, "plans to prosper you and not to harm you, plans to give you hope and a future. Then you will call on me and come and pray to me, and I will listen to you. You will seek me and find me when you seek me with all your heart."

JEREMIAH 29:11–13

After you suffer for a short time, God, who gives all grace, will make everything right. He will make you strong and support you and keep you from falling.

1 PETER 5:10, NCV

Guide me in your truth and teach me,
    for you are God my Savior,
    and my hope is in you all day long.

PSALM 25:5


Let us hold unswervingly to the hope we profess, for he who promised is faithful.

HEBREWS 10:23


But as for me, I watch in hope for the LORD,
    I wait for God my Savior;
    my God will hear me.

MICAH 7:7


May the God of hope fill you with all joy and peace in believing, so that by the power of the Holy Spirit you may abound in hope.

ROMANS 15:13, ESV


Why, my soul, are you downcast?
    Why so disturbed within me?
Put your hope in God,
    for I will yet praise him,
    my Savior and my God.

PSALM 42:11


Be joyful in hope, patient in affliction, faithful in prayer.

ROMANS 12:12

*WEEK*

26

I am thankful for...

# I am worried about...

_____

_____

_____

_____

_____

_____

_____

# I am praying for...

_____

_____

_____

_____

_____

_____

_____

*WEEK*
27

I am thankful for...

_____

_____

_____

_____

_____

_____

_____

_____

_____

_____

_____

_____

_____

_____

_____

_____

_____

# I am worried about...

_____

_____

_____

_____

_____

_____

_____

# I am praying for...

_____

_____

_____

_____

_____

_____

_____

_____

We pray for the big things and forget to give thanks for the ordinary, small (and yet really not small) gifts. How can God entrust great things to one who will not thankfully receive from Him the little things?

DIETRICH BONHOEFFER

# Pray Without Ceasing

WE ALL KNOW WHAT IT'S LIKE TO FEEL CAUGHT UP IN THE whirlwind of our daily lives. Our to-do list never stops growing, yet the days don't get any longer. There are certain times when prayer comes naturally—before a meal, before bed, when a loved one is suffering—but how can we pray consistently when it seems like we don't have the time to stop? At such times, consider the following verse: "Devote yourselves to prayer, being watchful and thankful" (Colossians 4:2). When we imagine unceasing prayer, we may envision ourselves speaking aloud to God wherever we are, possibly eliciting concerned glances from those around us. However, praying without ceasing means that we adopt a way of life in which every moment is a unique opportunity to connect with God.

We can pray when something specific happens for which we want to express our gratitude. *God, thank you for the promotion at work!* We might even pray when we're feeling particularly frustrated. *God, please give me the strength and grace to get through work today with my challenging teammate.* When we find it difficult to pray because of an unanswered prayer, it helps to admit our doubt to God. *God, help me trust you with all my longings.*

Eventually, this way of life will become instinctive, and you'll find yourself praying without ceasing. When you see someone in need, lift that person up in prayer, asking God to provide for his or her needs.

As we transition into this lifestyle, our burdens become less heavy. Our joy becomes more abundant. We find great assurance knowing that we are never alone, and the strength that we receive from our Heavenly Father is unmatched by anything else.

> Do not be anxious about anything, but in every situation, by prayer and petition, with thanksgiving, present your requests to God.
> *(Philippians 4:6)*

*WEEK*
28

I am thankful for…

_____

_____

_____

_____

_____

_____

_____

_____

_____

_____

_____

_____

_____

_____

_____

_____

## I am worried about...

_____

_____

_____

_____

_____

_____

_____

_____

_____

## I am praying for...

_____

_____

_____

_____

_____

_____

_____

_____

_____

*WEEK*
29

I am thankful for…

_____

_____

_____

_____

_____

_____

_____

_____

_____

_____

_____

_____

_____

_____

_____

_____

# I am worried about...

_____

_____

_____

_____

_____

_____

_____

_____

# I am praying for...

_____

_____

_____

_____

_____

_____

_____

_____

*WEEK*
## 30

## I am thankful for...

_____

_____

_____

_____

_____

_____

_____

_____

_____

_____

_____

_____

_____

_____

_____

_____

_____

I am worried about…

_____

_____

_____

_____

_____

_____

_____

I am praying for…

_____

_____

_____

_____

_____

_____

_____

_____

_____

## The Story Behind the Prayer

PASTOR AND MAN OF GREAT FAITH, MARTIN LUTHER KING JR. (born Michael Luther King) is known worldwide as a leader of the American Civil Rights Movement and as the visionary behind the famous "I Have a Dream" speech. To witness the power of prayer in his life, one need only look at a few of the accomplishments he made in the pursuit of bringing God's kingdom to earth. He became the president of the Southern Christian Leadership Conference, led the first peaceable demonstrations and marches in the history of modern America, spoke hundreds of times to further the cause of justice and equality, and became the youngest man to receive the Nobel Peace Prize.

His Prayer for the Church is only one of the many recorded prayers that continue to shape Christian culture and society as a whole. He prayed slightly varying forms of this prayer often during his time as a copastor of his grandfather's church, Ebenezer Baptist Church in Atlanta, and as a pastor of Dexter Avenue Baptist Church in Montgomery. This version was recorded in 1956, the same year the United States Supreme Court declared the practice of segregation on buses unconstitutional and the year before King began his formal leadership role in the American Civil Rights Movement.[5]

# Prayer for the Church

We thank thee, O God, for the spiritual nature of man. We are in nature but we live above nature. Help us never to let anybody or any condition to pull us so low as to cause us to hate. Give us strength to love our enemies and to do good to those who despitefully use us and persecute us.

We thank thee for thy Church, founded upon thy Word, that challenges us to do more than sing and pray, but go out and work as though the very answer to our prayers depended on us and not upon thee. Then, finally, help us to realize that man was created to shine like the stars and live on through all eternity. Keep us, we pray, in perfect peace; help us to walk together, pray together, sing together, and live together until that day when all God's children—Black, White, Red, Brown and Yellow—will rejoice in our common band of humanity in the kingdom of our Lord and of our God, we pray.

MARTIN LUTHER KING JR.

*WEEK*
31

I am thankful for...

_____

_____

_____

_____

_____

_____

_____

_____

_____

_____

_____

_____

_____

_____

_____

_____

_____

I am worried about…

_____

_____

_____

_____

_____

_____

_____

_____

I am praying for…

_____

_____

_____

_____

_____

_____

_____

_____

_____

*WEEK*
## 32

# I am thankful for…

_____

_____

_____

_____

_____

_____

_____

_____

_____

_____

_____

_____

_____

_____

_____

_____

I am worried about…

I am praying for…

God speaks
in the silence
of the heart.
Listening is
the beginning
of prayer.

MOTHER TERESA

## *Praying Scripture*

*DO YOU FIND YOURSELF PRAYING THE SAME WORDS REPEATEDLY?*
Has your prayer time become boring or uninspired? While we tend to think
of Bible reading and prayer as two separate spiritual practices, we can
combine them into one powerful practice of praying Scripture.

There are a few different approaches, such as praying the prayers
of Scripture word for word, personalizing portions of Scripture in your
prayers, or praying through various biblical topics.[6] Give this a try today.
Choose a Scriptural prayer such as Psalm 23, The Lord's Prayer in
Matthew 6:9–13, or Hannah's prayer in 1 Samuel 2:1–10, and let God's
Word refresh your spirit.

Another option is to search for and then pray through Bible verses that
speak to a specific need, such as hopelessness or anxiety (check out the
topical lists in this book). As you incorporate this practice into your prayer
life, may God's inspired Word strengthen your heart.

*WEEK*
## 33

## I am thankful for...

I am worried about...

_____

_____

_____

_____

_____

_____

_____

_____

I am praying for...

_____

_____

_____

_____

_____

_____

_____

_____

*WEEK*
## 34

## I am thankful for...

_____

_____

_____

_____

_____

_____

_____

_____

_____

_____

_____

_____

_____

_____

_____

_____

_____

# I am worried about…

_____

_____

_____

_____

_____

_____

_____

_____

# I am praying for…

_____

_____

_____

_____

_____

_____

_____

*WEEK*
## 35

## I am thankful for...

I am worried about…

_____

_____

_____

_____

_____

_____

_____

_____

I am praying for…

_____

_____

_____

_____

_____

_____

_____

_____

_____

# The Story Behind the Hymn

"*SAVED ALONE*" *WERE THE FIRST WORDS OF A TELEGRAM* that would forever change the life of Horatio Spafford. Tragedy, though, wasn't new to Spafford's life. Two years before, in 1871, the Great Chicago Fire had destroyed the city, including areas in which Spafford had heavily invested.

Life began to look up, and after two years of working with refugees from the fire, the family decided to vacation in Europe. Spafford was supposed to travel with his wife and four daughters, but business delayed him. He convinced them to go ahead of him to Paris. While crossing the Atlantic, their ship, the S.S. *Ville du Havre*, collided with the British iron sailing ship *Loch Earn*, and Spafford's four daughters perished. His wife, Anna, one of only twenty-seven survivors, managed to hang on to a piece of floating debris.

"Saved alone. . ." began the message from Anna that informed Horatio she was the only surviving family member.

He immediately left Chicago to be with his wife. While crossing the Atlantic, the captain pointed out to Spafford the area where his young daughters—eleven-year-old Anna "Annie," nine-year-old Margaret Lee "Maggie," five-year-old Elizabeth "Bessie," and two-year-old Tanetta—had perished. It was there, while in his pain and grief, Spafford penned the words that have since touched the hearts of millions.[7]

# It Is Well with My Soul

When peace, like a river, attendeth my way,
When sorrows like sea billows roll;
Whatever my lot, Thou hast taught me to say,
It is well, it is well with my soul.

*It is well with my soul,*
*It is well, it is well with my soul.*

Though Satan should buffet, though trials should come,
Let this blest assurance control,
That Christ hath regarded my helpless estate,
And hath shed His own blood for my soul.

My sin-oh, the bliss of this glorious thought!-
My sin, not in part but the whole,
Is nailed to the cross, and I bear it no more,
Praise the Lord, praise the Lord, O my soul!

For me, be it Christ, be it Christ hence to live:
If Jordan above me shall roll,
No pang shall be mine, for in death as in life
Thou wilt whisper Thy peace to my soul.

But, Lord, 'tis for Thee, for Thy coming we wait,
The sky, not the grave, is our goal;
Oh, trump of the angel! Oh, voice of the Lord!
Blessed hope, blessed rest of my soul!

And Lord, haste the day when the faith shall be sight,
The clouds be rolled back as a scroll;
The trump shall resound, and the Lord shall descend,
Even so, it is well with my soul.

HORATIO SPAFFORD (1873)

*WEEK*
## 36

I am thankful for...

I am worried about...

_____

_____

_____

_____

_____

_____

_____

_____

I am praying for...

_____

_____

_____

_____

_____

_____

_____

_____

*WEEK*
37

I am thankful for...

_____

_____

_____

_____

_____

_____

_____

_____

_____

_____

_____

_____

_____

_____

_____

_____

I am worried about...

_____
_____
_____
_____
_____
_____
_____

I am praying for...

_____
_____
_____
_____
_____
_____
_____
_____

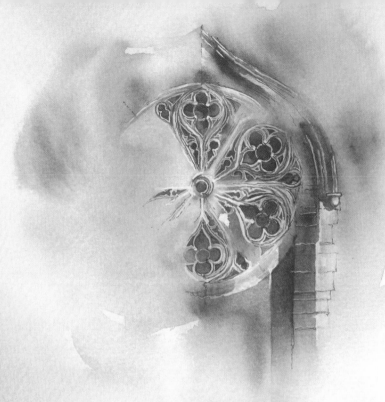

Create in me a pure heart, O God,
    and renew a steadfast spirit within me.
Do not cast me from your presence
    or take your Holy Spirit from me.
Restore to me the joy of your salvation
    and grant me a willing spirit,
    to sustain me.

PSALM 51:10–12

# Praying Through the Waiting

*HAVE YOU EVER GONE THROUGH A TIME OF ALMOSTS?*
These are times when you're praying for guidance or seeking the
Lord, and you feel at peace about moving forward in one direction,
things are lining up, and then...nothing. The job promotion, college
application, book idea, adoption, fundraiser, relationship, or
whatever-it-is goes nowhere. Instead, the answer you thought might
be *yes* turns into *wait*.

Continuing to pray throughout the waiting is often one of
the hardest things to do. It takes courage to wait and to remain
steadfast in prayer. Psalm 27:14 encourages us in this: "Wait for
the LORD; be strong and take heart and wait for the LORD." In
these times, be truthful and honest with the Lord. As you share
your frustrations, your pain, how deflated you feel, you'll find that
you are drawing closer to God. That's true intimacy, knowing your
burdens are in God's hands. Go to His Word to find reassurance
in His promises, such as "Be joyful in hope, patient in affliction,
faithful in prayer" (Romans 12:12).

The stories of people in the Bible who understood what it meant
to wait can also provide inspiration. Sarah longed for a child, and
despite trying to control the situation, she learned what it meant
to laugh and hold her baby in her arms. Hannah, who begged the
Lord for a son, was able to watch her son Samuel lead Israel as a
prophet and judge. Anna the prophet suffered greatly as a young
wife, but lived to see prophecy fulfilled in baby Jesus. The disciples,
Mary, and Martha grieved for three days after the death of Jesus,
wondering what was to become of them, but then encountered the
risen Christ.

Be brave in the waiting, for "The Lord is not slow in keeping his
promise....Instead he is patient with you" (2 Peter 3:9).

JOURNAL YOUR PRAYERS

*WEEK*
38

I am thankful for…

_____
_____
_____
_____
_____
_____
_____
_____
_____
_____
_____
_____
_____
_____
_____
_____
_____
_____

# I am worried about...

_____

_____

_____

_____

_____

_____

_____

_____

_____

# I am praying for...

_____

_____

_____

_____

_____

_____

_____

_____

_____

*WEEK*
39

I am thankful for...

I am worried about…

_____
_____
_____
_____
_____
_____
_____
_____

I am praying for…

_____
_____
_____
_____
_____
_____
_____
_____

*WEEK*
40

## I am thankful for...

_____

_____

_____

_____

_____

_____

_____

_____

_____

_____

_____

_____

_____

_____

_____

_____

_____

I am worried about...

_____

_____

_____

_____

_____

_____

_____

_____

I am praying for...

_____

_____

_____

_____

_____

_____

_____

_____

# Write Your Own Psalm

CONTAINING POETRY AND PRAYERS FROM DAVID, MOSES, and other Jewish writers, the book of Psalms is a unique collection that can help us give voice to our deepest longings and joys. Whether the psalmists are lamenting deep loss, crying out for God's deliverance, or celebrating the goodness of God, they are freely expressing their honest emotions. Reflect on the three passages below and then write your very own psalm on the next page. Do your best to articulate your feelings to God with authenticity.

How long, LORD? Will you forget me forever?
How long will you hide your face from me?
How long must I wrestle with my thoughts
and day after day have sorrow in my heart?

PSALM 13:1–2

As the deer pants for streams of water,
so my soul pants for you, my God.
My soul thirsts for God, for the living God.

PSALM 42:1–2

You, LORD, are forgiving and good,
abounding in love to all who call to you.
Hear my prayer, LORD.

—PSALM 86:5–6

*WEEK*
41

I am thankful for...

_____
_____
_____
_____
_____
_____
_____
_____
_____
_____
_____
_____
_____
_____
_____
_____

I am worried about...

_____
_____
_____
_____
_____
_____
_____
_____
_____

I am praying for...

_____
_____
_____
_____
_____
_____
_____
_____
_____

I am thankful for...

_____

_____

_____

_____

_____

_____

_____

_____

_____

_____

_____

_____

_____

_____

# I am worried about...

_____
_____
_____
_____
_____
_____
_____
_____

# I am praying for...

_____
_____
_____
_____
_____
_____
_____
_____
_____

Our prayers may be awkward. Our attempts may be feeble. But since the power of prayer is in the one who hears it and not in the one who says it, our prayers do make a difference.

MAX LUCADO

# *Praying Through Your Home*

WE ALL HAVE REGULAR HOUSEHOLD CHORES that are necessary
to keep our homes clean and tidy. Often, these thankless tasks become
mundane or burdensome. Why not redeem this time by praying specifically
as you move from room to room?[8] As you clean the kitchen or wash dishes,
pray for God's good gift of food. Pray that He will help you and your
family make healthy choices that honor Him. When you're tidying the
living room, give God thanks for the people He has brought into your life.
Pray for your friendships and that your home may be filled with God's
peace. While you're doing yet another load of laundry, ask God for joy
as you serve your family. Invite God into your daily routine through the
practice of prayer.

*WEEK*
## 43

## I am thankful for...

_____

_____

_____

_____

_____

_____

_____

_____

_____

_____

_____

_____

_____

_____

_____

_____

_____

I am worried about…

_____

_____

_____

_____

_____

_____

_____

_____

I am praying for…

_____

_____

_____

_____

_____

_____

_____

_____

I am thankful for...

_____

_____

_____

_____

_____

_____

_____

_____

_____

_____

_____

_____

_____

_____

_____

# I am worried about...

_____

_____

_____

_____

_____

_____

_____

_____

# I am praying for...

_____

_____

_____

_____

_____

_____

_____

_____

*WEEK*

45

I am thankful for...

_____

_____

_____

_____

_____

_____

_____

_____

_____

_____

_____

_____

_____

_____

_____

_____

_____

# I am worried about…

---

# I am praying for…

---

# The Story Behind the Prayer

IGNATIUS OF LOYOLA WAS BORN IN 1491, one of thirteen
children born to a family of minor nobility in the Basque region
of Spain. His mother passed away shortly after his birth and
he was raised by the local blacksmith's wife. As a boy, Ignatius
was inspired by adventure stories about the chivalrous knights
of Camelot and the epic poem *The Song of Roland*. In fact, he
dreamed of becoming a famous knight who would seek romance
and adventure far from the small village where he grew up.

At seventeen, Ignatius left home and joined the army. He went
on to serve as a knight for Antonio Manrique de Lara, the second
Duke of Nájera, and he became known as the "servant of the
court" for his tremendous skills in leadership and diplomacy. He
prevailed through many duels and military battles before being
gravely injured by a cannonball in 1521.

During his convalescence, Ignatius began reading religious
texts about Jesus and the lives of the saints, which were the
catalyst for his profound spiritual conversion. He was inspired to
devote himself to God and went on to found the Society of Jesus,
also called the Jesuits. In 1524, he completed an influential book
called *The Spiritual Exercises*, written to help readers discern
God's presence in their daily lives and the precursor to today's
thirty-day devotionals.

In his Prayer for Generosity, we can see the evidence of
Ignatius's fascinating life story. He had experienced true
transformation and instead of the personal glory he had pursued
in his youth, his sincere desire was to serve the Lord without
counting the cost or seeking a reward.[9]

# Prayer for Generosity

Dearest Lord, teach me to be generous;
Teach me to serve thee as thou deservest;
To give and not to count the cost,
To fight and not to seek for rest,
To labour and not to seek reward,
Save that of knowing that I do thy will.

---

ST. IGNATIUS OF LOYOLA (1491–1556)

*WEEK*

# 46

## I am thankful for...

_____

_____

_____

_____

_____

_____

_____

_____

_____

_____

_____

_____

_____

_____

_____

_____

_____

_____

# I am worried about...

_____
_____
_____
_____
_____
_____
_____
_____
_____

# I am praying for...

_____
_____
_____
_____
_____
_____
_____
_____
_____

*WEEK*
47

I am thankful for...

I am worried about...

_____
_____
_____
_____
_____
_____
_____
_____
_____

I am praying for...

_____
_____
_____
_____
_____
_____
_____
_____
_____
_____

Whatever you ask in
my name, this I will do,
that the Father may be
glorified in the Son.
If you ask me anything in
my name, I will do it.

JOHN 14:13–14 (ESV)

# When We Don't Have the Words to Pray

WE HAVE ALL EXPERIENCED TIMES IN OUR LIVES when the circumstances seem so dire that we don't know how to pray. When our grief is too deep, our pain too fresh, when we don't have the strength to form the words, we can hold on to this promise: "The Spirit helps us. We do not know what we ought to pray for, but the Spirit himself intercedes for us through wordless groans. And he who searches our hearts knows the mind of the Spirit, because the Spirit intercedes for God's people in accordance with the will of God" (Romans 8:26–27).

Praying through Scripture not only gives us the words we might not have but reminds us who God is by recalling His faithfulness, love, and promises. We can fully rely on these truths:

I praise you because I am fearfully and wonderfully made;
> your works are wonderful,
> I know that full well. (PSALM 139:14)

The LORD will fight for you; you need only to be still. (EXODUS 14:14)

Your word is a lamp for my feet,
> a light on my path. (PSALM 119:105)

Ask and it will be given to you; seek and you will find; knock and the door will be opened to you. For everyone who asks receives; the one who seeks finds; and to the one who knocks, the door will be opened. (MATTHEW 7:7–8)

*WEEK*

48

## I am thankful for…

---
---
---
---
---
---
---
---
---
---
---
---
---
---
---
---

I am worried about…

_____
_____
_____
_____
_____
_____
_____

I am praying for…

_____
_____
_____
_____
_____
_____
_____

*WEEK*
49

I am thankful for…

# I am worried about...

_____

_____

_____

_____

_____

_____

_____

_____

_____

# I am praying for...

_____

_____

_____

_____

_____

_____

_____

_____

*WEEK*

## 50

I am thankful for...

I am worried about...

_____

_____

_____

_____

_____

_____

_____

_____

_____

I am praying for...

_____

_____

_____

_____

_____

_____

_____

_____

Even though I walk through the valley of the shadow of death,
    I will fear no evil,
for you are with me;
    your rod and your staff,
    they comfort me.

PSALM 23:4, ESV

Praise be to the God and Father of our Lord Jesus Christ,
the Father of compassion and the God of all comfort, who
comforts us in all our troubles, so that we can comfort those in
any trouble with the comfort we ourselves receive from God.

2 CORINTHIANS 1:3–4

The Lord defends those who suffer;
    he defends them in times of trouble.

PSALM 9:9, NCV

Therefore if you have any encouragement from being united
with Christ, if any comfort from his love, if any common
sharing in the Spirit, if any tenderness and compassion, then
make my joy complete by being like-minded, having the same
love, being one in spirit and of one mind.

PHILIPPIANS 2:1–2

Remember your word to your servant,
    for you have given me hope.
My comfort in my suffering is this:
    Your promise preserves my life.

PSALM 119:49–50

Those who try to hold on to their lives will give up true
life. Those who give up their lives for me will hold on to
true life.

MATTHEW 10:39, ESV

The righteous person may have many troubles,
    but the LORD delivers him from them all.

PSALM 34:19

For our light and momentary troubles are achieving for us
an eternal glory that far outweighs them all. So we fix our
eyes not on what is seen, but on what is unseen, since what
is seen is temporary, but what is unseen is eternal.

2 CORINTHIANS 4:17–18

I remain confident of this:
    I will see the goodness of the LORD
    in the land of the living.
Wait for the LORD;
    be strong and take heart
    and wait for the LORD.

PSALM 27:13–14

And we know that in all things God works for the good
of those who love him, who have been called according
to his purpose.

ROMANS 8:28

*WEEK*
51

I am thankful for…

_____

_____

_____

_____

_____

_____

_____

_____

_____

_____

_____

_____

_____

_____

_____

I am worried about…

_____

_____

_____

_____

_____

_____

_____

_____

_____

I am praying for…

_____

_____

_____

_____

_____

_____

_____

_____

_____

*WEEK*
## 52

## I am thankful for...

I am worried about...

_____

_____

_____

_____

_____

_____

_____

_____

I am praying for...

_____

_____

_____

_____

_____

_____

_____

*SIT IN A PLACE* you would not usually pray, whether that's on a mountain, in a shopping mall food court, or at a coffee shop. Write down the thoughts or prayers that come to mind.

_Any concern too small to be turned into a prayer is too small to be made into a burden._

CORRIE TEN BOOM

*REFLECT ON*
a key relation-
ship in your
life that is
strained or dif-
ficult. Ask God
to soften your
heart toward
that person.
Then, journal
some ideas for
how you could
be intentional
in breaking
through the
conflict.